Are You DESIRABLE *Or* AVAILABLE?

OLUSEGUN AKINKUGBE

ARE YOU DESIRABLE OR AVAILABLE?

ISBN: 978-1-9161791-6-5

Published by:
Gracehouse Publishing
56, Gosport Road, Walthamstow,
London, United Kingdom, E17 7LY

Unless otherwise indicated, all Scripture quotations are taken from the New King James Version (NKJV) of the Bible.

CONTENTS

FOREWORD

As someone who has the privilege to positively influence thousands of people through various platforms in several countries and cities around the world. I have come to an honest realisation that being able to do what I do is not just because I am available; it because I am desirable – VALUED!

The honest truth is that I did not get to this place in just one moment. There have been times and seasons in my life that I was confused, broken and not a lot of people thought much of me or any possibility of good coming from me. Like many individuals today, in finding acceptance I made myself available to everyone who cared and didn't cared; still, that didn't make me the guy everyone gathered around or talked about.

Products get bought off the store shelve; services get

patronised not just because they are offered but because people or organisations actually need them. The truth is that life opportunities serve us in this very manner, in the sense that the edge we have over our contemporaries or as a businessperson over our competitors is not a function of existence but relevance.

To become desirable requires self-discovery, intentionality, personal growth and keen focus. What makes you different is what makes you needed, which means you and me must become comfortable with our individual make-up or design. It then becomes a thing of necessity to become the best version of oneself through consistent rigorous self-improvement. As this becomes the case, you gradually begin to harness your God-given abilities to add value to your surroundings which then increases your impact then desirability.

If there is anything that is true; it's the author Olusegun Akinkugbe who I have known and witnessed in nearly a decade of our friendship, ministry and business partnership not only grow himself but hundreds of others not just to exist but truly live. The author has never been mistaken of who he is; an important issue he addressed which is the subject of discovering one's personal identity as an integral element for an individual to leverage their innate abilities and being able to contribute positively to their immediate as well as the extended environment.

Again, as he has rightly stated in this book that *"Everybody has been given a level playing field as a gift from God called life"*. It is therefore important that utmost attention should be given to how we play as supposed to just playing; everyone of us must play in the best possible way for our lives to count and not just be counted in the numbers of those who existed and gone.

This book is filled with enriching wisdom and nuggets that is guaranteed to cause a progressive shift in the thought processing of its readers, and I'm truly grateful it is coming at a time it is most needed due to the prevalent culture in our societies today. A lot of people today need to be reoriented that nothing precious is found on the surface; there is a process of one having to dig deep, refine and proper presentation to achieve desirability. I am confident that as you read through each page of this book, you will find truths and inspiration that will motivate you in your journey to the best version of yourself.

Thank you, Olusegun (Psegs). This is definitely a masterpiece and timely too!

Apostle Femi Adun
President, *Eagle World Outreach*

INTRODUCTION

I have always been a student of excellence and achievement. Maybe because I saw myself that way. When I was younger I felt that I ought to belong to an exclusive club of those others wanted to be like. I was attracted to Charisma, excellence in presentation, outstanding substance, great grooming and dressing. I would walk to the front row after events such as concerts, church conferences, seminars just to see how it felt like to be in front, walk by the speaker, entertainer or preacher. I would watch theirs mannerisms, graceful movements, speech and internalize it. At home in my room I would visualize what it would feel like and what I needed to do to get there.

In the month of November 2000 I heard Reverend Sam Adeyemi say at the Foursquare National Convention " you cannot travel within and stand still without, you can only attract who you have become". That was my watershed moment. I knew I had to transform into this people or rather into the version of myself I would admire. The journey had to start within and so I plunged into a life long discipline(this is still who I am today) of studying my Bible yearly, studying relevant books in my profession (then practicing as a lawyer I would read a monthly report every month and later at least two weekly reports a month). I studied Christian literature John C Maxwell, Bishop Oyedepo, Mike Murdock and consumed the late great Dr Myles MUNROE. My car became a mobile lecture hall Paul Adefarasin, Sam Adeyemi, Bishop Oyedepo, Myles MUNROE, TD Jakes etc.

It's been almost twenty years now I don't see myself as an expert but a life long learner. Still studying, still listening, still praying, still traveling within and truly I now realize I am mostly now in front. I see those young men and women loitering around me, watching me, smiling quietly and I remember, I reach out to them, engage them and tell them you remind me of me.

This book lays out what I applied and I'm still applying to ensure the journey continues. It's the key to becoming your best version of yourself. You don't have to be only Available you can be Desirable. Have a blessed read.

CHAPTER 1

WHICH ONE ARE YOU

If I brought two plain white T-shirts to you, both of the same material, same colour, and no brand attached, how much would you be willing to pay for the shirts? Some of you would say £2.00, some £1.00 or even 50p. What if both shirts were still of the same colour, same fabric but one had the Nike tick on it, how much would you be willing to pay for it. I can feel your interests growing; some of you would say £10 or £15, wow just because of the tick, what if we were to place a man on a horse playing polo on the shirt (Ralph Lauren), how much would you pay for it, £20 or £25?

So what exactly happened here, that would cause the same kind of shirt to move from costing £1 to £25, why will a person be more willing to pay so much for a brand. The answer is simple, both shirts are available, but one is more desirable as a brand.

So I thought of other scenarios when a pastor calls a parishioner (let's take the name of Greg for the parishioner). The pastor calls Greg the single good looking young man, who works in a financial institution, earns good money, very fervent and heads the choir of over 40 single young ladies, yet he's single unattached and searching. So the pastor says to him, young man what is the problem? You are leading over 40 single young ladies, yet you are still praying for a wife, what is your problem? Can't you find a young lady in this ocean of godly women to marry? Greg softly replies pastor there is no lady to marry in this choir. What is he really trying to say, he means pastor they are all available but I don't find them desirable for me.

Anita another young lady has been accused by her mother of being too picky, the only man in her life is Jesus Christ. Will Jesus marry you is the constant question, why won't you pick from your several suitors, what is your problem. Mother she is only saying that they are available but not desirable.

In my last scenario, Kingsley has decided to travel to the village to get a wife. He has been in the city for several years serving faithfully in the church as an usher. Over this period of time he has approached 12 young ladies and not one said yes. Now out of frustration, he is preaching a gospel that single ladies in the church are stuck up, yet four of his friends who will be going with him to the village got married in the last year to four of the women who turned him down. Deep down, he knows there is something wrong somewhere. It must be his step mother who bought him soap the last time he travelled (superstitious voodoo), she has bewitched him with a very negative aura, that the three deliverance sessions he has attended has not resolved. Here is the truth Kingsley you are available but not desirable.

We could go on and on creating different scenarios, but there is an underlying question here, why are so many people attaining the marriageable age but are not successful in finding marriage. A part of the issue, which I will attempt to tackle in this book, is the conflict of people being available but not being desirable.

Everyone desires the desirable over the available. Amongst companies, during recruiting sessions the reason a company would bypass several applicants and invite only a few for the interviewing process, is because the CVs of the few are more desirable than the several that are available. Life is for the desirable, before getting to the deep spiritual questions of conviction when it comes to marriage, the truth is people will give the desirable a chance before considering the available options.

The available is the norm, freely given, sold a dime a dozen, the general. The truth is that no one wants to settle for that, we all desire the exclusive and the unique because that is how the creator made us. Hence as a person grows financially and increases in spending power, they stop purchasing off the rack and start to order specially made and designed items. We do this because it is the nature of man to desire what is rare. These items are specially prepared by the manufacturer over time to satisfy the consumer's ultimate taste. The same law applies to relationships, to be desirable we must be prepared to meet specific tastes and we also desire a specific need to be met. That is what this book is about; it's about preparing us to be uncommon in thinking, action, outlook or appearance but becoming unique in God. As a matter of fact it is a travesty for a Christian to be common Psalm 139:14 ***"I will praise thee; for I am fearfully and wonderfully made: marvellous are thy works; and that my soul knoweth right well.***

We ought to be so in touch with our uniqueness that we all stand apart from each other in the calling, graces and personality that God has blessed us with. When trained lawyers walk into their offices to the world they are all lawyers, but amongst themselves they are all different. Different specialities, different niches and different value attached to every individual. So it is also with us, we have been created by God as unique and our intrinsic value as individuals comes from tapping into that uniqueness. When we appreciate our uniqueness in God then desirability will flow out of us. Paula White the evangelist was told when she was a child that she would never amount to much because she was a talkative, however now her talking gift has become a gift to millions around the world. So stop being common and maximise your uniqueness.

Even though everyone appreciates and desires the

desirable, it is not everyone who can attract the desirable. Only the desirable can attract desirable people like themselves. We all attract what and who we are. This force of attraction is not necessarily about looks but who we are on the inside. We can only have what we have been built to have. Let's take for example Fortune 500 companies. They are desirable, everyone, if wishes were horses would want to work for them, but that is not the reality. They only employ the best in their different fields of specialization. These are people who have shown competence and skill in certain areas where they require employment. So it is with relationships, we all desire to court and marry the desirable; however we must become the desirable ourselves. We must show that we have what it takes to bring value to the relationship. Nobody employs us because we want the salary, but because of the value and the contribution we will bring to the organisation. So also no one will be interested in us because we want to be seen with them, claim ownership status over them, ride in their cars, spend their money or pose with them. People are attracted to people who add value to them spiritually, emotionally, mentally and physically.

So my question is this, what contribution and values have you acquired, to give to another person? No one complains that a company does not give him or her a job if they lack the skills to work for the company. Stop complaining about rejection if you are yet to acquire the skills to make a relationship work. You studied for several years to become competent professionally or vocationally, you heard several things and were continuously poised to hear more because you were hungry to get the right information, process this information, internalise it make it a part of you and then display it as an area of competence. I am alarmed at the arrogant ignorance of several people who believe you don't have to study anything regarding relationships and marriage. How can we be so ignorant, man is such a complex creature, still being studied and yet we assume that we understand human beings enough to handle them in marriage and relationships even when we do not really understand ourselves?

Friends it is the people according to Daniel 11:32 *"And such as do wickedly against the covenant shall he corrupt by flatteries: but the people that do know their God shall be strong and do exploits"* who will do exploits in marriage. Even so it is the people who know what to do with the knowledge they acquire who can be successful in navigating through the storms of relationships and marriage. Search for the knowledge, acquired knowledge increases desirability. Ecclesiastes 8:1" *Who is the wise man? And who knoweth the interpretation of a thing? a man's wisdom maketh his face to shine and the boldness of his face shall be changed."*

CHAPTER 2

CULTIVATING DESIRABILITY

Desirability can be likened to a man walking down a street of several gardens, some are bare, some overgrown, some cultivated, some bland. Most people will walk past the bare gardens, the overgrown, and the plain but will stop to admire the cultivated gardens. Now these cultivated gardens were like all the others but the owners chose to work on them. The owners chose to give them particular attention. Everybody has been given a level playing field it is the gift from God called life. A lot of times we may feel some people are more gifted than others, but the truth is God has given us everything we need for our lives in Christ Jesus. 2 Peter 1:*3* ***"According as his divine power hath given unto us all things that pertain unto life and godliness, through the know ledge of him that hath called us to glory and virtue."*** We should not compare ourselves with others but rather should maximize everything that we have. 2 Corinthians 10:12 ***"For we dare*** *not make ourselves of the number, or compare ourselves with some that commend themselves: but they measuring themselves by themselves, and comparing themselves among themselves, are not wise*. The distance between where we are currently and where we desire to be is dependent on how well we have invested our TIME in cultivating our gifts. We are where we are today because of how we used our time yesterday, and the destination of tomorrow will be a result of the stewardship of our time today.

To cultivate means to grow and develop those latent qualities in a seed till it becomes everything it can be. Nobody wants to eat a seed but we all love to eat fruits from trees. Your uncultivated self is a seed; your desirable self is you being a tree full of fruit. Cultivation of self and talents are the steps we take to translate from seed form to fruit form.

Desirability is also likened to refinement. Refined products are worth much more than crude products. Diamonds in there crude forms look like stones, when refined they shine like stars. Without being refined people would not spend half the amount they spent on diamonds refined if they were sold crude. Friend you are like a diamond, God created you complete and extremely desirable, but you can't leave that desirability dormant within. You have got to work it out, work out the gifts, abilities, and strengths and discover those things. The desirable people of this earth are not better than us; they just chose to cultivate themselves. Now everyone is chasing the refined product, so know that if you choose to work on yourself you will become desirable in every facet of life including marriage.

So when we say cultivation is growth we mean a steady development over a period of time. Real growth takes time. We always have to cast the vision to become whatever we desire to become long before we become it. We have to intentionally apply ourselves to a process over a period of time. The greatest satisfaction of achievement is the growth and development not the event. We learn from people who developed over time not one night wonders. Those who applied and committed themselves to the process are the people we celebrate and learn from. Jim Rohn an American speaker said "set goals not to just get to them but for what they will make of you." So if my goal is to become a millionaire, it should not be about acquiring the millions in my account because I could lose that, but rather it should be about the man I will become while acquiring it, for I can never lose that.

So Pastor what is the gist. You give yourself time to become the man every woman desires or the woman everyman desires. Proverb 18:22 ***"Whosoever finds a wife finds a good thing and obtains favour of the Lord."*** It takes time to become a wife or husband. Not all women or all men are wives or husbands. It takes time to become one. To become a wife or husband one must be an asset, and it takes time and investment to become one. It will involve a commitment to learning and growth over a period of time.

It takes time to be a husband and father, having a baby or being sexually active does not make you one, responsibility does. It takes time to build that ability till it has the right response mechanism to life's issues. We can all be desirable it just takes time to be committed to the process. I want to take you on a little journey of certain things that God showed me would help us transition from just being available to becoming desirable.

1 Samuel 16:18 " ***Then answered one of the servants, and said, Behold, I have seen a son of Jesse the Bethlehemite, that is cunning in playing, and a mighty valiant man, and a man of war, and prudent in matters, and a comely person, and the LORD is with him***" this is my inspiration for writing this book. Each of the qualities of David are the traits that we will be studying in the next few chapters to help cultivate the growth to become desirable.

CHAPTER 3

IDENTITY

"Behold, I have seen a son of Jesse the Bethlehemite"

No one has the right to determine another person's criteria to be labelled a success or a failure. Man sets these criteria based on his own opinion of what success and failure should be regardless of what the creator's plan is. An example could be for instance who determines academic excellence. When I was still in the secondary school you needed 5 credits to show you were intelligent enough to graduate from the secondary school. Who determined that it would be five credits, I am not saying that the criteria was wrong but I am just saying that it was not Gods criteria and so does not determine my destination and arrival into the realm of success or failure. A successful gospel recording artist whilst in music school failed twice and was told he would never amount to anything, Paula White the televangelist was told by her grade school teacher that she would not succeed because she talked too much, who would ever consider that two of this generations greatest speakers would have lisp in speaking TD Jakes and John Maxwell.

Why am I saying all this, because we cannot afford to let the opinion of others form our identity and opinion of ourselves. Many people perceive themselves not being desirable because of the opinion they feel others have of them. As a matter of fact the opinion we feel others have of us is actually the opinion we have of ourselves. Number 13:33 "***And there we saw the giants, the sons of Anak, which come of the giants: and we were in our own sight as grasshoppers, and so were we in their sight.***" The way we allow people to treat us is a mirror of how we perceive ourselves, and can I tell you that that perception and identity is very wrong. We can not afford to form our identity based on what our peers, parents, colleagues or bosses think; No our identity is rooted and grounded in God who created us and he alone knows all what he has placed in us.

Mans opinion varies from one location to another. In Europe beautiful models are slavishly skinny, in Africa they are voluptuous. Some men desire slim women; others desire curvy women (you should see my wife). Some women are attracted to light skinned men others love the tropical deep hue. Some people are attracted to height others to short and stocky. A person who allows his or her opinion of themselves be determined by the opinions of people will never be happy.

I studied law in Nigeria as a first degree, we were taught that the more we remembered verbatim of what the lecturer taught or dictated the better we were as students. So we became skilled at cramming. When I came to the United Kingdom for my Masters degree I failed my first exams because unlike in Nigeria my lecturer here did not want me to reproduce what I had been taught but he wanted my own personal evaluation. So the same exam I failed in the UK would have given me high scores successful in Nigeria. Hence my conclusion, that man's standard is usually developed by culture, development and even demand, it does not take into consideration the gifts that God has given to you. Your perception of yourself, your looks, academics, skills and talent must not come from man but from God who gave it to you.

That our God given identity remains intact regardless of the experiences we may have had in our lives. If I have a £50 note in my hand and it falls in a dirty toilet bowl, I would have two options, I could be so disgusted that I flush it away or I could take it out, clean it up, spread it out to dry and still spend it because despite the terrible experience it's been through, it has not lost its purchasing power. This analogy applies to all of us. There are times we go through certain debilitating events in our lives that the enemy tries to use to scare us, and make us believe our life is no longer as valuable as God made it. What we need to understand is that the value God placed in us and his identity in our lives cannot be taken away by such events. In the world of entertainment so many of the heroes we look up to went through terrible experiences that could have defined them negatively and changed their identity in life. Yet these ones have chosen to hinge their value on God's gifting in their lives and have continued to make their lives matter. Joyce Meyer was sexually abused yet she rose from it to become one of the world's most inspirational speakers. Donnie Mcclurkin has won several awards and is considered universally as one of the most powerful voices in gospel music. He was raped as a child and struggled for years with his sexuality and yet he rose above that to become one of the greatest gospel artists ever. Les Brown was labelled mentally challenged and slow as a child yet he rose to become a successful law maker and foremost motivational speaker and life coach. Abraham Lincoln failed several times before becoming President; Tyler Perry came from an abusive background. These group of people had issues, they still wear the scar of these experiences like the pound that fell in the toilet however they don't doubt the value of their identity in God.

To be desirable we need to have an assurance of our identity in God and realise that regardless of what people feel about us and how they try to classify us and put us down, it is God's opinion about us that really matters and the truth is that God does not make anything worthless.

No one can define us accurately, man will only define according to experience or some reference they have. Even Jesus had his identity misconstrued by his disciples some called him a prophet others called him Elijah, meaning they labelled him by something they had seen before. As a pastor I have heroes and mentors that I have listened to and sat under. When someone tells me I remind them of any of these I am flattered but I am not and will never be any of them, I am myself. The only person who interpreted Jesus rightly was Peter and he did it by the Holy Spirit. It is only the Holy Spirit who can truly reveal yourself even to you talk less of others. They truth is that we don't even know ourselves. When I refer to the name Alex Ferguson people in my generation will call him an extremely successful coach, in an earlier generation he was known as a mediocre footballer not in the class of the Maradonas or Peles. However the truth is that he is both depending on what angle you look at him from.

Friend you are who God has made you your identity is in God. He alone defines me. Desirability comes as a function of us appreciating ourselves for who we are not based on any man made standards and improving to be the best of who we are. So for instance I work out regularly not to be like Arnold Swarchzneggar, Usain Bolts or the strongest man alive but to become the strongest, fittest and gifted that I can be.

When I spend time praying and fasting I don't want to be the next E.A Adeboye, David Oyedepo, Creflo Dollar or Sam Adeyemi, I want to be the most anointed and effective me there can be. Godliness with contentment is great gain. If I am not content with who God has made me I will not maximise what he placed in me. The fact that I am about 6 feet 3 inches and can't play basketball does not mean my height is wasted, I am constantly grateful for areas where the height serves rather than despise my limitation.

The more I appreciate who God has made me as a person the more desirable I will feel and it is only a matter of time before people change their perception about me.

CHAPTER 4

SKILL

"That is cunning in playing"

Many years ago I attended a concert with a lady (we had been at this heart issue for a while) I was trying to date her. Whilst at this concert i was dazed by the performance of the musicians particularly the keyboardist who was also a vocalist. At the end of the evening a friend introduced him to us. We exchanged pleasantries, told him how incredible his renditions were and were about to move on, when I noticed the body language of the girl I was with towards this musician. I had been trying all evening to make her laugh, smile and generally create a conducive atmosphere for us to enjoy each other's company. However I noticed that the same girl I had been sweating to make laugh and smile was just giggling like a drunkard to everything this "dude" was saying. Obviously she was more attracted to him or at least regarded him better. Now watching him objectively there seemed to be a glow to his smile, a look of self assured confidence and esteem that comes from a sense of accomplishment and proficiency in his craft. That day I learnt another lesson, confidence and what contemporary English speakers call "swagger" is a function of skill in ones chosen area of life.

I have always known that it takes confidence to get a job, start a business or marry a spouse. Confidence is that intangible quality that commands incredible results from unlikely people. Ever seen a really beautiful lady getting married to a guy that just made you wonder how? Let me give you the answer- CONFIDENCE. Or some guy attends an interview he was not really qualified for but still gets hired – CONFIDENCE. Confidence is that nebulous substance that creates an aura around those who carry it. There was a time I thought confidence was just a gift from God. I thought you either had it or didn't have it, but over the years and having conversed with a few "superconfident" people I have come to understand that confidence is acquired from gaining mastery and skill in that area of life that matters to us.

Self-awareness is about understanding one's self, ones sense of value, ones core belief and inner aspiration. When we become proficient in our core then we will exude the confidence that attracts. As a child Dennis was raised in a spiritual home, to very loving and secure parents. His hidden desire was to become a successful musician in the mould of Smokie Norful. So as he grew his parents encouraged him to play and learn music. He always felt extremely alive when in church on Sunday for music ministrations. He was also academically sound, and so chose to study accounting. In the university he was extremely popular as musician in his fellowship and all campus fellowships. His gifts as a musician exposed him to so many ministers, lecturers, the Vice Chancellor and eventually the State Governor who attended an event he performed at. On graduation his parents advised him to get a job at a bank. How much can you earn from being a musician, who is Smokie Norful anyway. So for a period of four years he concentrated on banking, but no matter how hard he tried he was just a good accounting banker. No genius to him, he was like every other person. Amongst his peers there were stars in the field of banking but he was not one of them. Even the girl he desired turned him down for really no plausible reason. Eventually due to harsh financial constraints the bank had to let some staff go and he was unfortunate to be one of them.

Unemployed having nothing to do and needing some money he took up a job at a church as a music director. Within three months his genius was back, he had built the choir from ten to fifty members. The church had grown greatly because everyone wanted to go to the church with the fantastic choir. Within the year the choir released an album; he became sort after and became a consultant to other choirs. His confidence soared, then he met Courtney a very sophisticated spiritual lady he would have thought was out of his league, but based on his proficiency in his skill he had grown in confidence and esteem.

Whatever skill you have at your core that is what you work on. Not what parent's want, but what your heart cries after. Developing yourself in this area till it becomes an area of competence. The moment we know we have what it takes to fulfil our dreams (confidence means I know I have what it takes) that becomes our launching pad for all of our other pursuit. Hence in my opinion the greatest desire for a single person should not be for marriage, but for a lifetime vision from God. Developing the skill to facilitate that vision will command the right person to be attracted to our lives.

Developing skill in our purpose is simply bringing out the star in each of us. Everyone has a treasure in them, which must be expressed, the expression of that treasure, gift or ability and its development is what is called the refinement of the person. When we arrive at our refined selves then we start exuding confidence and self esteem. Hence it is always important that we have an avenue to express our gifting and ability Jim Rohn the great American Philospher said "you can start by working full time on your job and part time on your fortune" till the reverse becomes the order. Working on ones fortune is working on ones core gift or ability, that thing given by God to profit with. That's why leisure is extremely important for that is where we work on our gifts. Places like churches, drama and music clubs, personal art exhibitions, just find an avenue to express your gift and value it till it adds value.

In the Bible Michal was in love with David because he had found his purpose and excelled in it. Zara Phillips the oldest granddaughter of Queen Elizabeth of England recently got married to Martin Tindall the rugby player. Why will a royal marry a commoner, because the commoner has shown he is uncommon by excelling and being skilful in his gift? Now he has the confidence and will to not be intimidated being married to a princess. We can also develop in our gift till we are so skilful that it exudes a confidence in our core that spread to all parts of our being.

VALOUR

"and a mighty valiant man"

Life is full of battles. Challenges abound everywhere for Christians. Jesus said in this world we would suffer tribulation but be of good cheer I have overcome the world. These challenges are not only world issues like climate change, national issues like bad economies but also personal issues like relationships gone bad. However God has given us the ability to overcome challenges. The bible says in **1Jn 4:4 that "....greater is he that is in me than he that is in the world."** Simply meaning that regardless of how bad the challenge is that I face, I have what it takes to overcome.

Regarding challenges in our relationships there are times when we suffer disappointments, rejection via a broken courtship or an unfavourable response to a proposal. At times like this our confidence is injured, we feel sad, our expectation of ourselves suffers a depletion and we feel less than we really are. We know that if we are to come into Gods desire for our marital bliss we ought to persevere and move ahead, but we are wounded, and know that any movement we initiate presently will only lead to greater anguish, so what do we do.

At times like this the most important thing to do is to feed off our relationship with God. Listen when man tells you; you are not wanted that seed of rejection seeks to plant a seed of low self-esteem. It takes our oneness with God and our knowledge of this to restore our esteem and help us remember that the most important personality in the universe loves us, we don't need the validation of any other love to be whole. Rejections and disappointments paint the lying pictures that maybe certain things, jobs, school or people are too good for us. However Rom8:32" *He that spared not his own Son, but delivered him up for us all, how shall he not with him also freely give us all things*? Makes me understand that if God gave Jesus to die for me, and Jesus was God's best, given for me, then there can be nothing in this world that can be too good for me. So friends at times like this we feed off the love of God to refill our well of inspiration. I suffered a rejection which years later I thank God for, because it was more of a redirection. I remember that after that experience I sought to improve myself on all fronts. I started by studying the Bible rigorously, then I read books, I also learnt to pray. Then I heard my pastor then Paul Adefarasin tell of a story of a rejection he suffered also.

I was inspired, something leaped in me, I looked at this successful man of God and said to myself I deserve the best and now years later that experience was a blessing in disguise and honestly I have the best. My wife is a super babe not only by Christian standards but on any level. I fed off God's love and it restored my belief to forge ahead knowing good things were ahead.

While I was working on myself I decided to be more proficient in my calling as a music minister, teacher of the word, as well as in my profession as a lawyer. The more I improved, the more my confidence grew to face the challenge of seeking and finding love again. Why did this matter so much to me?

Let me explain. When a man meets an old friend after a long time they exchange pleasantries and try to catch up with each other. They ask questions that mainly go vocational and not really relational. A man hardly ever stops on just saying I am now married, I have two daughters, and I live in Glasgow with my wife. Most times we go beyond this to our vocation by saying I am a Vice President at a blue chip cooperation, I also pastor a church in this city doing quite well. I'm sure you know I am now married and have two lovely daughters. Women on the other hand are different talking more about their kids, husband and mothers in law. Why? They are more relational. A man has a greater launching pad of being able to face life when he is secure in his vocation (fulfilment, financial stability, and progress). Women on the other hand could be professionally astute and fulfilled but they are more of nurturers who receive the greater fulfilment from those in their lives. Hence a man with a happy marriage and good kids but no job would be miserable, whilst a woman with a very good job but suffering in her relationships is not happy. Now don't get me wrong, I am not being chauvinistic and saying that women are not professionally minded, not at all. As a matter of fact I see them excelling the more in that regard nowadays. Women excelling in the marketplace and God made them nurturers. Hence why the devil attacks women the more on the home front than in the market place. Men vice versa are finding it harder to get a job hence leading to frustration in the home. I love my wife and daughters, but l also knows that something about the work of my hands makes me feel capable as a provider and protector of my home.

Based on this understanding of man I see my key role as that of helping my wife settle properly into the relationships around her. Particularly with her parents, my parents, our siblings because as a wife she receives a lot of gratification from how well she handles this relationships. Getting this right will enable her to handle other relationships till she is termed a woman of virtue and good character. For most women? fulfilling that criteria are based on well-handled relationships than professional proficiency.

In marriage the woman's role is to help the man build, nurture and achieve his purpose. There is no greater sense of fulfilment in a man than when he is walking in his destiny and excelling in it. It creates peace and security for him. Underachievement and frustration are the greatest causes of marital strife on the part of men. The issue is not that you are earning more as a woman, but in the fact that his job is frustrating, he has no security or fulfilment in it and it makes him feel less than whom he is. A man like Sir Dennis Thatcher who was married to Baroness Margaret Thatcher the former female British Prime Minister was secure in his marriage, yet his wife was the most powerful woman in the World. Why? Because he was content. He was a decorated military man, highly accomplished who retired as a major with honours; he was an oil consultant, a business mogul. As a matter of fact he sponsored his wife's study to become a lawyer.

Another example of such a man is Stedman Graham,Oprah Winfrey's long time partner(I know they are not married, but I am talking of men not intimidated by female success). He is an entrepreneur, corporate consultant and motivational speaker, a very wealthy man in his own right, who is not intimidated by Oprah's wealth and influence.

This notion that money breeds respect is false. The bible story of the king Ahaseurus found in the book of Esther establishes this. The Bible says he ruled 127 Provinces, threw a party for 180 days, then a dinner for seven days. Isn't that crazy rich and powerful, yet the Bible says when he summoned his wife she refused to answer him in public, such disrespect. Eventually she lost her place due to the pressure placed on him by leaders in the kingdom.

A key lessonfor me was that his wealth could not guarantee he commanded his wife's respect. Rather she embarrassed him publicly. The truth is before you can embarrass a king publicly you must have been doing it privately. A king, wealthy, powerful but without honour from his wife. He did not show himself a capable man worthy of honour. He gave her no reason to honour him. He lived for parties and pleasure, and did nothing to command his wife's respect. There is so much more to honour beyond money, for men it stems from our fulfilment in our calling and vocation, for women it stems from how well we nurture in the home and then the market.

CHAPTER 6
A MAN
OF WAR

***M**att 11:12"........the kingdom of God suffereth violence and the violent take it by force."* A Christian's call is a call to fight the good fight of faith. We must be ready to fight for what we know is ours. Nothing worthwhile comes cheap on to the earth. Our adversary the devil is on a lifelong pursuit stop us from enjoying the fullness of every good thing God has for us, particularly in the area of marriage, courtships and relationship. Nothing of value is ever free, valuable things must cost us something.

More often than not Christians believe that once God says he has given us something there will be no resistance however that is quite the opposite. ***Matt 13;21 [20] But he that received the seed into stony places, the same is he that heareth the word, and anon with joy receiveth it;***

[21] ***Yet hath he not root in himself, but dureth for a while: for when tribulation or persecution ariseth because of the word, by and by he is offended.*** From this verses we can infer that because God promises certain things does not mean we won't fight for it, fight for the courtship, career, ministry, marriage plan. No we are called to fight hence the bible's description of us as soldiers of Christ. Our call as soldiers is to fight to establish the kingdom of God. However it will be a battle because there is another kingdom on the earth that does not agree with the kingdom of God.

What is the kingdom of God- it's God's agenda and plan for the earth in our generation and we all play a vital part. As the seed of Abraham God's word to our great father still stands ***Gen 12:3"...through you all the families (nations) of the earth shall be blessed."*** Hence through our lives God has ordained that certain people will be blessed, part of that blessing is the ability to overcome the challenges of life that the devil will bring across our ways to have a testimony that will encourage others.

Abraham's greatest claim to fame is that at the age of a hundred and Sarah at ninety were able to conceive and have a son. Hence any barren couple that hear this testimony are encouraged to fulfil the kingdom agenda for them, which is that none of us shall be barren.

The Bible says in ***1 Tim 1:18"...according to the prophecies which went before thee that thou by them mightiest war a good warfare.*** " Friends the purpose of prophecy is to keep your hope and faith alive so you can wage a good warfare. We have to keep the right attitude in the midst of challenges and be able to believe God against all odds that God will do what he promised despite the odds. In ***Rom 4:18-21 "who against hope believed in hope, that he might become the father of many nations, according to that which was spoken, so shall thy seed be? And being not weak in faith, he considered not his own body now dead, when he was about a hundred years old, neither yet the deadness of Sarah's womb. He staggered not at the promise of God through unbelief, but was strong in faith, giving glory to God and being fully persuaded that what he had promised, he was able to perform.***

If God made you or myself a promise, our job is to be violent in our resolve regarding heaven's ability to perform what has been promised. Violence is about being consistent in thought believing God for what he has said. Tenacious and ready to stand by God's word. When God promises he does not need our help to fulfil his word to us. What he requires from us is absolute trust. For a lot of us as believers our way of helping God is by resorting to certain low level human practices that do not line up with the integrity of God's word. Abram resorted to impregnating Hagar Sarah's maid because in their mind they were helping God. Several of us resort to such ungodly practices, which only go on to contaminate the blessing God intended.

We cannot resort to carnal measures of lying on our resumes and creating false expectations on the part of employers to get career advancement when we do not possess such skill. As a pastor I have several times counselled young ladies not to resort to demeaning practices such as bedding and feeding to keep a man they are not yet married to, also young men resorting to borrowing cars, clothes, even flats to impress ladies is ungodly.

Friends God only needs what is in your hands to fight your wars for you. After all it was not a gun, submachine, submarine, sword, spear, bow or arrow that brought down Goliath. No it was a simple sling and a stone. Very crude equipment but mighty when used by our God. What then does that say, God only needs what you have available (which is what he has given you) to get you where he is taking you.

For the single person waiting on God for the desired promise, the best resolve is to commit the promise and keep on moving on the path of righteousness (that is doing what is right not resorting to questionable methods that do not glorify God). Joseph had no hand in his emancipation from prison; it was all by the hand of God. So shall it be for you, when God will bring you into the fulfilment of his desire. Just to encourage someone when I was chasing my wife for marriage it seemed like for a long time I could not breakthrough to get to her. But all of sudden after a trip she made to London, the moment she came back things changed. If you ask me what I did differently till today I cannot say, but what I know is that now God's promise regarding my marriage has been fulfilled in that regard.

PRUDENT IN SPEECH

Col 4:6 "Let your speech be always with grace seasoned with salt, that ye may know how ye ought to answer every man."

Several years before I got born again as a University undergraduate, I had a friend (a lady) who one day in a conversation with me said she once had a crush on me before we eventually became friends. This lady was extremely gorgeous, and as a testosterone driven young man I was disappointed she would now settle at being my friend and not explore the possibility of a more beneficial relationship.

She told me she had nursed the crush for months until the day we eventually met. She said I was having a conversation with some friends of hers, and that while she listened to the conversation, her distant impression of me was much better than the disappointment she felt from hearing my conversation. I was shocked by such a terrible testimonial of my "gift of my garb". I had to inquire about what I had said, and her response was that I was a shallow, silly, opinionated young man that completely repulsed any feeling of intrigue she might have nursed earlier. For years after, that conversation bothered me particularly whenever I met someone new., I eventually discovered the above scripture and a statement that said "garbage in garbage out". Though I am now married, I am still extremely careful about what I feed my thoughts on because I understand that out of the abundance of what I feed my mind and spirit on, my mouth speaks. To ensure that my speech is very sound, my thoughts must be sound and what I feed myself on must be sound.

Prudence of speech extends beyond wise sayings, to even speaking properly with the right vocabulary and diction. Just hang around any group of young people and listen to their conversation and it almost sounds like a foreign language with little snippets of English. Most of the language is broken and the vocabulary is limited. When the conversation ought to be formal, the limited vocabulary is more obvious. Young people sound frustrated, they constantly repeat words such as "it's like, as per or you get" and then go on to blame the education system. Yes the education system is flawed, but it is not just because of what is being taught in schools but rather the biggest deficit in the culture of young people now is that there is no desire for personal development by reading widely. In my opinion the greatest key to the sophistication of thought patterns is in the study and reading of sound literature. It starts with the bible; you cannot study God's word and not develop God like thoughts. Also I advocate for sound Christian literature, personal development books and great educative fiction like John Grisham. These materials impart wisdom and exposure, magazines like TIME, NEWSWEEK and the ECONOMIST also add to this.

Knowledge is bought and acquired; when it is properly digested and is applicable it becomes wisdom, which the Bible says makes a man's face to shine. It attracts, a person who speaks properly and wisely carries a force of attraction that men are compelled to respect.

In the Bible we are told the story of Solomon the king said to have been the wisest man that ever lived, and the Queen of Sheba.

The Bible says this woman travelled a long distance from a distant country because she had heard of Solomon's wisdom and she came with hard questions for him. The Bible says he answered all her questions even better than she expected till she testified to his greatness. Every young person desires the best in life, to be paid the most, to be the most respected and sought after. Friends can I tell you that you cannot command that level of respect till you have something to offer people around you including the person you desire. Acquire wisdom and become prudent in speech.

Some of the truly most desired men to have ever lived were desired because of their wisdom. Huge crowds followed Jesus and several women ministered to his need because he had something to offer them. The Bible itself says in **LK 4:16"....as his custom was he went into the synagogue on the Sabbath day and stood up to read".** He was a man of study; let the thirst for wisdom form our habit to start thirsting for wisdom so that our words will become seasoned with salt. *Isaiah 55:1 " Ho everyone that thirsteth, come ye to the waters, and he that hath no money;come ye buy and eat;yea come buy wine and milk without money and without price. Wherefore do ye spend money for that which is not bread? And ye labour for that which satisfieth not? Hearken diligently unto me and eat ye that which good,and let your soul delight in fatness".*

As I said earlier in this book if you want the best you must become the best, to become the best you must study the best and the way they think. In another Biblical story we are told that David was about to take vengeance on a certain Godless man by the name of Nabal.

According to the story in *1 Samuel 25:1-42 " And Samuel died; and all the Israelites were gathered together, and lamented him, and buried him in his house at Ramah. And David arose, and went down to the wilderness of Paran.*

[2] *And there was a man in Maon, whose possessions were in Carmel; and the man was very great, and he had three thousand sheep, and a thousand goats: and he was shearing his sheep in Carmel.*

[3] Now the name of the man was Nabal; and the name of his wife Abigail: and she was a woman of good understanding, and of a beautiful countenance: but the man was churlish and evil in his doings; and he was of the house of Caleb.

[4] And David heard in the wilderness that Nabal did shear his sheep.

[5] And David sent out ten young men, and David said unto the young men, Get you up to Carmel, and go to Nabal, and greet him in my name:

[6] And thus shall ye say to him that liveth in prosperity, Peace be both to thee, and peace be to thine house, and peace be unto all that thou hast.

[7] And now I have heard that thou hast shearers: now thy shepherds which were with us, we hurt them not, neither was there ought missing unto them, all the while they were in Carmel.

[8] Ask thy young men, and they will shew thee. Wherefore let the young men find favour in thine eyes: for we come in a good day: give, I pray thee, whatsoever cometh to thine hand unto thy servants, and to thy son David.

[9] And when David's young men came, they spake to Nabal according to all those words in the name of David, and ceased.

[10] And Nabal answered David's servants, and said, Who is David? and who is the son of Jesse? there be many servants

now a days that break away every man from his master.

[11] Shall I then take my bread, and my water, and my flesh that I have killed for my shearers, and give it unto men, whom I know not whence they be?

[12] So David's young men turned their way, and went again, and came and told him all those sayings.

[13] And David said unto his men, Gird ye on every man his sword. And they girded on every man his sword; and David also girded on his sword: and there went up after David about four hundred men; and two hundred abode by the stuff.

[14] But one of the young men told Abigail, Nabal's wife, saying, Behold, David sent messengers out of the wilderness to salute our master; and he railed on them.

[15] But the men were very good unto us, and we were not hurt, neither missed we any thing, as long as we were conversant with them, when we were in the fields:

[16] They were a wall unto us both by night and day, all the while we were with them keeping the sheep.

[17] Now therefore know and consider what thou wilt do; for evil is determined against our master, and against all his household: for he is such a son of Belial, that a man cannot speak to him.

[18] Then Abigail made haste, and took two hundred loaves, and two bottles of wine, and five sheep ready dressed, and five

measures of parched corn, and an hundred clusters of raisins, and two hundred cakes of figs, and laid them on asses.

[19] And she said unto her servants, Go on before me; behold, I come after you. But she told not her husband Nabal.

[20] And it was so, as she rode on the ass, that she came down by the covert of the hill, and, behold, David and his men came down against her; and she met them.

[21] Now David had said, Surely in vain have I kept all that this fellow hath in the wilderness, so that nothing was missed of all that pertained unto him: and he hath requited me evil for good.

[22] So and more also do God unto the enemies of David, if I leave of all that pertain to him by the morning light any that pisseth against the wall.

[23] And when Abigail saw David, she hasted, and lighted off the ass, and fell before David on her face, and bowed herself to the ground,

[24] And fell at his feet, and said, Upon me, my lord, upon me let this iniquity be: and let thine handmaid, I pray thee, speak in thine audience, and hear the words of thine handmaid.

[25] Let not my lord, I pray thee, regard this man of Belial, even Nabal: for as his name is, so is he; Nabal is his name, and folly is with him: but I thine handmaid saw not the young men of my lord, whom thou didst send.

[26] *Now therefore, my lord, as the LORD liveth, and as thy soul liveth, seeing the LORD hath withholden thee from coming to shed blood, and from avenging thyself with thine own hand, now let thine enemies, and they that seek evil to my lord, be as Nabal.*

[27] *And now this blessing which thine handmaid hath brought unto my lord, let it even be given unto the young men that follow my lord.*

[28] *I pray thee, forgive the trespass of thine handmaid: for the LORD will certainly make my lord a sure house; because my lord fighteth the battles of the LORD, and evil hath not been found in thee all thy days.*

[29] *Yet a man is risen to pursue thee, and to seek thy soul: but the soul of my lord shall be bound in the bundle of life with the LORD thy God; and the souls of thine enemies, them shall he sling out, as out of the middle of a sling.*

[30] *And it shall come to pass, when the LORD shall have done to my lord according to all the good that he hath spoken concerning thee, and shall have appointed thee ruler over Israel;*

[31] *That this shall be no grief unto thee, nor offence of heart unto my lord, either that thou hast shed blood causeless, or that my lord hath avenged himself: but when the LORD shall have dealt well with my lord, then remember thine handmaid.*

[32] *And David said to Abigail, Blessed be the LORD God of Israel, which sent thee this day to meet me:*

[33] *And blessed be thy advice, and blessed be thou, which hast kept me this day from coming to shed blood, and from avenging myself with mine own hand.*

[34] *For in very deed, as the LORD God of Israel liveth, which hath kept me back from hurting thee, except thou hadst hasted and come to meet me, surely there had not been left unto Nabal by the morning light any that pisseth against the wall.*

[35] *So David received of her hand that which she had brought him, and said unto her, Go up in peace to thine house; see, I have hearkened to thy voice, and have accepted thy person.*

[36] *And Abigail came to Nabal; and, behold, he held a feast in his house, like the feast of a king; and Nabal's heart was merry within him, for he was very drunken: wherefore she told him nothing, less or more, until the morning light.*

[37] *But it came to pass in the morning, when the wine was gone out of Nabal, and his wife had told him these things, that his heart died within him, and he became as a stone.*

[38] *And it came to pass about ten days after, that the LORD smote Nabal, that he died.*

[39] *And when David heard that Nabal was dead, he said, Blessed be the LORD, that hath pleaded the cause of my*

reproach from the hand of Nabal, and hath kept his servant from evil: for the LORD hath returned the wickedness of Nabal upon his own head. And David sent and communed with Abigail, to take her to him to wife.

[40] And when the servants of David were come to Abigail to Carmel, they spake unto her, saying, David sent us unto thee, to take thee to him to wife.

[41] And she arose, and bowed herself on her face to the earth, and said, Behold, let thine handmaid be a servant to wash the feet of the servants of my lord.

[42] And Abigail hasted, and arose, and rode upon an ass, with five damsels of hers that went after her; and she went after the messengers of David, and became his wife."

The Bible in this story described Abigail as a beautiful woman, however she proved that her beauty extends beyond her appearance. This woman having heard of her husband's inappropriate behaviour and sensing the danger prepared victuals herself to take to David to dissuade him from executing his plan.

The first thing I noted was that even though her husband Nabal was even described by the Bible as a fool, Abigail protected him. This woman protected her home and family. Then on approaching David the Bible makes us understand that she dissuaded him not just by providing food for him and his men but that she spoke words of wisdom that stirred him in a different direction. She spoke into his future; she read him perfectly and made him understand that his actions ought to be executed in the light of his destiny and not in the confusion of his circumstance. Eventually at the demise of her husband Nabal, David took her to become his wife, not because of her beauty but because he knew he needed her wisdom.

Whoever will desire us must desire the wisdom heaven has placed in us and not just our looks and economic ability. Those things can fly away but our wisdom abides and stays with us through our lifetime.

CHAPTER 8

COMELY

The Bible describes David as being comely in person meaning he was not hard to look at, he was actually attractive to behold. I have come to the conclusion that looking good is not a function of having money to purchase expensive clothing, or wearing designer clothes, but it is a state of being so much in communion with God that his peace, confidence and radiance is reflected through our own visage. It is a state of comportment that is rooted in a place beyond human ability.

When we study his story in scripture, David was coming from the field where he was taking care of his father's sheep, but something about him commanded the aura of a king. I have heard several times that it is not about a person being found in the jungle, but it is about the jungle not taking root in the person. David was not defined by his circumstances the fact that he was rooted and grounded in God meant that his esteem and worth come from a place beyond his situation and circumstance. In **Psalm 42:11** *"Why art thou cast down, O my soul? and why art thou disquieted within me? hope thou in God: for I shall yet praise him, who is the health of my countenance, and my God.* Friends our confidence about life can't be defined by what we do or don't do rather it is defined by God and the value he has placed on us.

In Gen 39:1-3 "[1] And Joseph was brought down to Egypt; and Potiphar, an officer of Pharaoh, captain of the guard, an Egyptian, bought him of the hands of the Ishmeelites, which had brought him down thither.

[2] And the LORD was with Joseph, and he was a prosperous man; and he was in the house of his master the Egyptian.

[3] And his master saw that the LORD was with him, and that the LORD made all that he did to prosper in his hand."

We are told the story of Joseph as a slave in Potiphar's house. The Bible says that he was so prosperous in the grace of God that his master set him over the entire household. The Bible further goes to say that he was successful that his master's wife sought to seduce him and sleep with him. We all say that this was due to good looks, but good looks flow from within beyond external features. We are all wonderfully and fearfully made, however the reason some seem more attractive than others is the inner state of beauty and confidence that emanates from who God has made you. Joseph was a slave but in the eyes of this woman he was more attractive than his master, her husband because of the aura he carried, the aura that would take him from slavery, to prison and, to the palace.

Another wonderful example was Esther who became Queen of Persia. This lady was a slave, who contested in a beauty pageant with a several other beautiful virgins. She was chosen, not because she was the most beautiful, best-spoken, most social pedigree but rather she was chosen because she found favour based on the presence of the person within. We have got to draw our beauty and radiance from our relationship with God before we can embark on anything else.

Despite all of the above to be truly comely attractive and desirable there are certain physical laws we should take into cognisance.

1 Sam 17:6-7 "⁶ And it came to pass, when they were come, that he looked on Eliab, and said, Surely the LORD'S anointed is before him.

⁷ But the LORD said unto Samuel, Look not on his countenance, or on the height of his stature; because I have refused him: for the LORD seeth not as man seeth; for man looketh on the outward appearance, but the LORD looketh on the heart."

It is God that looks at the heart, not man so if we want to be addressed properly by people we must mind our appearance.

1). *1 Peter 2:9 " But ye are a chosen generation, a royal priesthood, an holy nation, a peculiar people; that ye should shew forth the praises of him who hath called you out of darkness into his marvellous light:"*

Dress and look the way you want to be addressed. We are royalty in God; hence we must dress and carry ourselves as royalty not in carnal pride but in humility of knowing whom God has made us. Christian ladies cannot afford to dress tacky flaunting body parts or guys sagging jeans rather we must look like people who want to be taken seriously as ambassadors of God's Kingdom. It is unbecoming for a princess to look like a cheap prostitute and for a prince to look like a thug. We must dress in a way that is fashionable but yet depicts us as children of God.

2) We must dress appropriately for each occasion this will make people comfortable in communicating with us. When we dress out of place it causes discomfort for who ever we are with, because we attract unnecessary attention. I remember years ago, going to the beach where I saw a guy take the lady to the beach for a picnic. She looked the part of someone having fun at the beach even to her cute little basket and umbrella. The guy on the other hand, looked out of place, he was wearing a suit and carried a big bible. He was sweating and refused to do away with the jacket and

tie, so we started to suspect the shirt must have been stained. The entire outing was counterproductive because, his appearance only created the greater discomfort, by making the lady unnecessarily uncomfortable.

When in church dress the part of one going to worship God, looking right based on the community we find ourselves. In the UK amongst Caucasians dressing up for Sunday service is a casual affair. So when in such an environment dress appropriately comfortably and to fit into the environment.

3) Wear what fits you. There is nothing as ridiculous as a big bellied guy in a body hugging shirt or tight fitting suit. Nor as bad as a skinny looking lady in extremely big clothes. As people we should know what fits us.

I am on the big side and so I am careful about what I wear. I have skinny knocked knees and so you will never see me in the name of summer or heat wearing shorts in public. Neither will I wear extremely fitted attires because the look will be counterproductive. We cannot afford to be fashionably dumb, but we must always look our best with what fits our physique.

There is no ultimate physique in my opinion; it just about knowing what to wear to suits you, particularly amongst ladies who are big boned and very curvy. That's a blessing; there is no need to envy a skinny model, rather you should dress in what fits your physique, ooze with the confidence of who you are in God and carry yourself with the aura of royalty.

The last tip i will give in this regard is that of exercising. Now you may be thinking what is he talking about, he just said there is no ideal physique so what is the purpose of exercise. Well if that is your mindset let me educate you.

The Bible says bodily exercise profiteth little...but it still profits and it is that profiting we will maximise.

1). Exercise strengthens our cardio and skeletal muscle system. This helps you carry your body weight better. In this instance hence you will walk with a better upright gait that exudes confidence. This is the reason why athletes look really nice it is because their skeletal muscle system is right, not necessarily the six pack or V shape. If you start exercising regularly and your body tones up, your clothes will sit better on you and you will move with a smarter gait.

2) Exercising also increases our body metabolism and burns fat. Fat is the excess weight that is not needed in the human body. When in excess it weighs us down and causes us to look and move sloppily. Your body was given to you by God, so you should do everything possible to ensure that it is kept in the best possible shape to the glory of his name.

3) Exercise relives stress by producing body chemicals that bring the body into a physical and emotional balance. When these chemicals are released from the pores and a shower is taken to wash off the sweat it helps the body to

rest better. Hence you will wake up more alert and energetic to combat life. Nothing is as attractive as a positive aura.

With all these things and benefits gained from exercise we can conclude that they all conclude in long life and prosperity.

THE GOD FACTOR

The measure of a person's prosperity is not in what they own, possess or control but I would rather say that the measure is in the presence of God that such a person carries about. Jesus referred to this in Luke 12:15.

Hence when we look through the scriptures at the great men and women of God who made a difference, (above all else including physical or material prosperity) they commanded an incredible dimension of God's presence that ensured that they lived in a different class from everyone else. The Bible referred to Abraham as the father of faith and indeed he proved the character and mettle of his faith beyond regular understanding. It is naturally impossible for a hundred year old man and a ninety year old woman to have a child. It was not by their strength or ability but it was just a manifestation of the presence and power of the God they carried.

Isaac the son of this very old man of faith planted in a famine very adverse circumstances and made maximum profit. His prosperity was not tied to the economic buoyancy of where he was, or the fertility of the soil because it wa sin famine, but the manifestation of the God he carried.

Abraham's grandson by the name of Jacob also manifested God's presence despite the oppression and ill treatment he suffered from his boss Laban. Despite the disadvantage Laban tried to confine him to his prosperity was tied to the revelation he received from the angel sent by the God he worshipped.

Finally in this context Joseph Abraham's great grandson despite being sold into a land of slavery rose to prominence in a foreign land. He got into trouble for rejecting his master's wife's desire for an illicit affair (guys money is not the only source of attraction) and was tossed into prison. From prison because he was still being a blessing by helping others who were in the same dire straits, he eventually rose to become Prime Minister of Egypt by interpreting Pharaoh's dream. How could a non national, ex convict and slave rise to such prominence? By the power of the God we heard he carried.

You may ask what has all this got to do with a single person who wants to be desirable. The presence of God is the biggest force of desirability. The presence of God is so powerful that he will make people seek us out from impossible places. It was this presence that was manifested in the life of John the Baptist that caused men to leave the city to go meet him in the wilderness. Your location cannot stop the right suitor from coming; all we need is the presence of God.

In New Testament parlance the presence of God is represented by the Holy Spirit, the spirit of truth and grace. He is called the Spirit of Truth and Grace because he is the only one who can teach us the truth about ourselves and whoever desires marriage or a relationship with us. He will also help us come into Gods perfect will in marriage which we don't deserve that's his grace. The Holy Spirit makes things clear and brings certain things we need to change and improve upon to our attention. The Holy Spirit gives us his ability to be able to do things we normally would not be able to do. I remembered when I was chasing my wife, she did not seem to be interested initially and when normally would have gotten to a point where I would have backed down I just felt constrained to keep at it. Years later whenever I recall those times I know I did not chase her by my power but his, because left to me I would have given up turned back.

Friends the bible is very interested in our marriages but without God being the prevalent factor there will be no marital bliss. God brought Eve to Adam, even before he knew what he wanted. He knew he was alone, knew he needed something but nothing he named could be called his bone or his flesh. It could be so with many of us, we need someone, we don't know who and everyone around us is being named, then please wait on God like Adam slept and he will bring yours into your space, his Spirit will bless you with the gift of recognition in the name of Jesus. Amen